AF270224

Adélie Penguin

by Grace Hansen

abdobooks.com

Published by Abdo Kids, a division of ABDO, P.O. Box 398166, Minneapolis, Minnesota 55439.
Copyright © 2022 by Abdo Consulting Group, Inc. International copyrights reserved in all countries.
No part of this book may be reproduced in any form without written permission from the publisher.
Abdo Kids Jumbo™ is a trademark and logo of Abdo Kids.

Printed in the United States of America, North Mankato, Minnesota.

102021

012022

 THIS BOOK CONTAINS RECYCLED MATERIALS

Photo Credits: Getty Images, iStock, Shutterstock

Production Contributors: Teddy Borth, Jennie Forsberg, Grace Hansen
Design Contributors: Candice Keimig, Victoria Bates

Library of Congress Control Number: 2021940132
Publisher's Cataloging-in-Publication Data

Names: Hansen, Grace, author.

Title: Adélie penguin / by Grace Hansen

Description: Minneapolis, Minnesota : Abdo Kids, 2022 | Series: Antarctic animals | Includes online
    resources and index.

Identifiers: ISBN 9781098209377 (lib. bdg.) | ISBN 9781098260088 (ebook) | ISBN 9781098260439
    (Read-to-Me ebook)

Subjects: LCSH: Adélie penguin--Juvenile literature. | Adélie penguin--Behavior--Juvenile literature. |
    Penguins--Juvenile literature. | Zoology--Antarctica--Juvenile literature. | Antarctica--Juvenile
    literature.

Classification: DDC 591.709113--dc23

Table of Contents

Antarctica

Antarctica is the southernmost continent. Nearly all of Antarctica is covered by ice. It is one of the coldest, driest, and windiest places on Earth. But some amazing animals still live there!

Africa
South America
Antarctica
South Pole
Australia

Adélie Penguins

There are 18 **species** of penguins in the world. Just two live in Antarctica year-round. The Adélie penguin is one of them.

Adélies live on the continent and on some of the surrounding islands. They spend their winters feeding offshore. In the spring, they can be found on the rocky **coasts**.

Adélies are medium-sized penguins. They are around 27 to 29 inches (68.5-74 cm) tall. They weigh up to 13 pounds (5.89 kg).

Adélie penguins have black and white feathers. Their faces are black, except for the rings of white feathers around their eyes.

Like all penguins, Adélies are
master swimmers. Their bodies
are shaped to move easily
through water. Their strong
wings, webbed feet, and tails
help them **propel** and steer.

Baby Adélie Penguins

Breeding season begins in October. **Colonies** of Adélies can be found onshore in ice-free areas. The penguins build their nests and line them with stones.

Females lay two greenish-white eggs. Males and females take turns keeping the eggs warm. The eggs hatch after about 35 days.

19

While one parent keeps the chicks warm, the other hunts. After two or three weeks, the **colony's** chicks gather in **nursery** groups to stay safe. Soon, they will be ready to swim and hunt!

21

More Facts

- Adélie penguins mainly eat fish, krill, and other tiny shrimplike animals.

- Adélie penguins may be small, but they are brave and tough. They will take on bigger animals, and even people, to protect themselves and their young.

- Adélie penguins were named by French explorer Jules Dumont d'Urville. He named the birds after his wife, Adéle.

Glossary

breeding season – a period of time when animals come together to have young.

coast – the area of land next to the ocean.

colony – a group of animals of the same type living closely together.

krill – a very small, shrimplike animal that lives in the open seas.

nursery – a place where young animals gather to grow and be cared for.

propel – to push or drive forward.

species – a group of living things that look very much alike, share a similar name, and can have young with one another.

Index

Visit **abdokids.com** to access crafts, games, videos, and more!